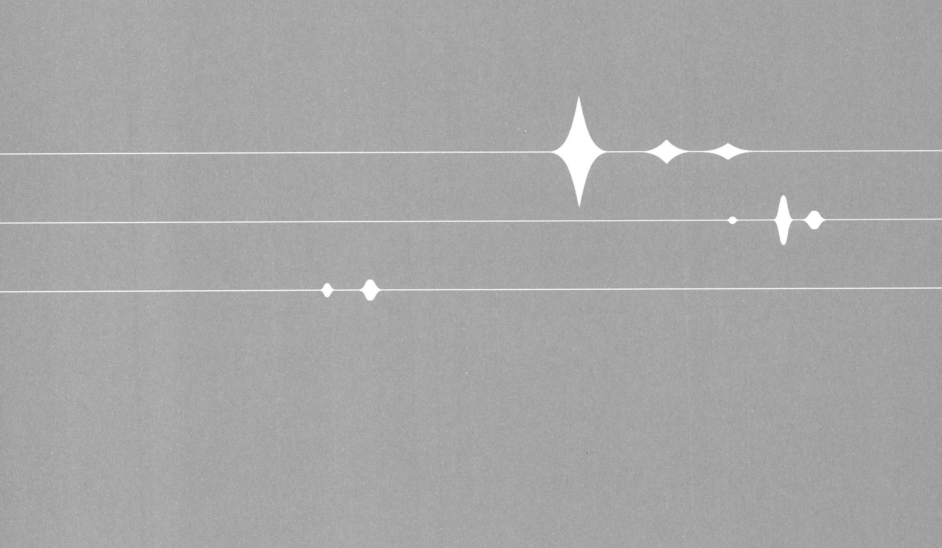

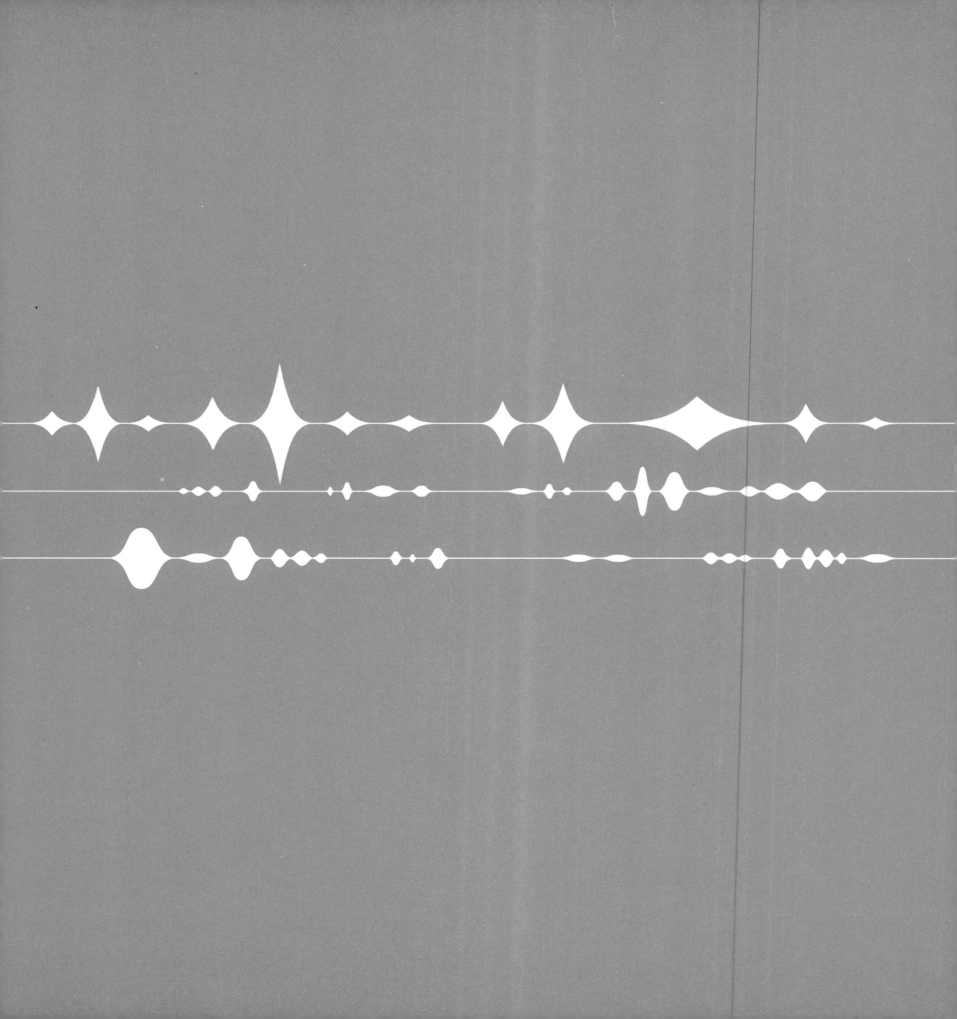

SOUND

Shhh . . . Bang . . . POP . . . BOOM!

Romana Romanyshyn and **Andriy Lesiv**

Translated by **Vitaly Chernetsky**

A Handprint Book

In the beginning it may have been quiet.

But then it became loud. The universe filled with sounds.*

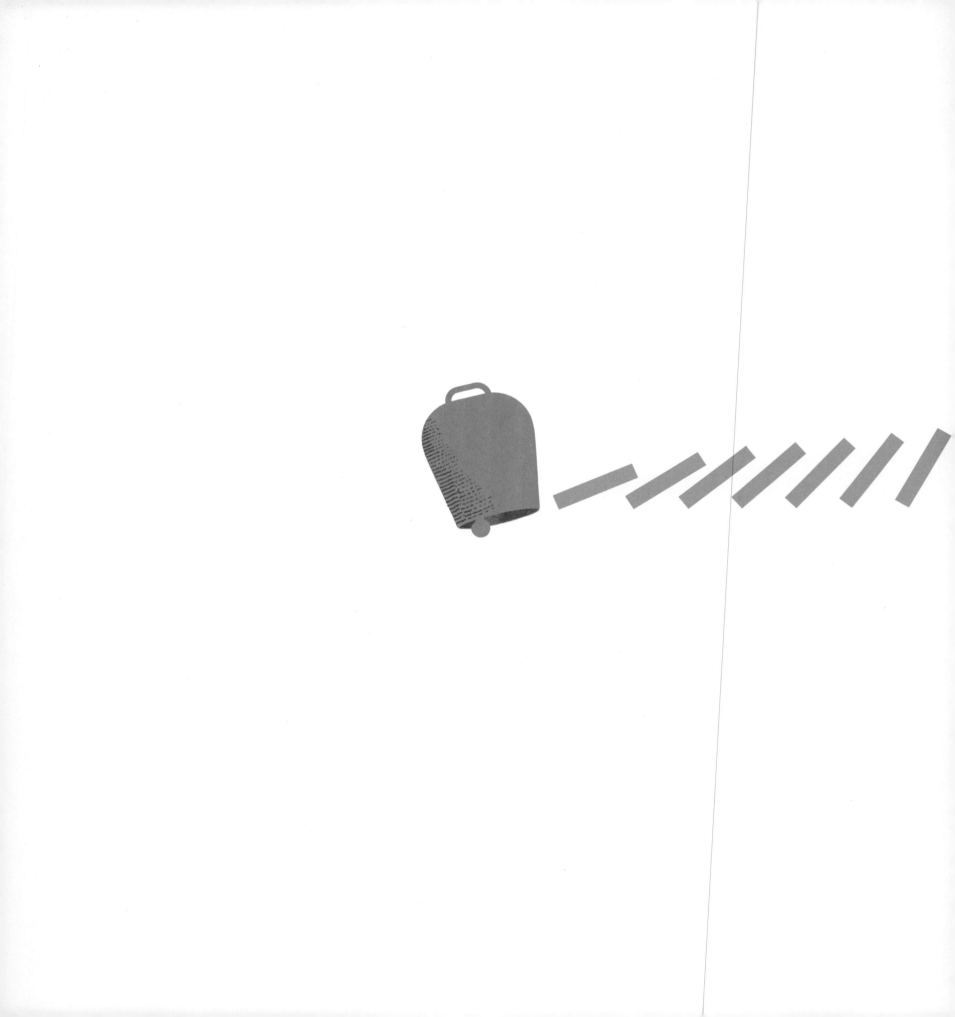

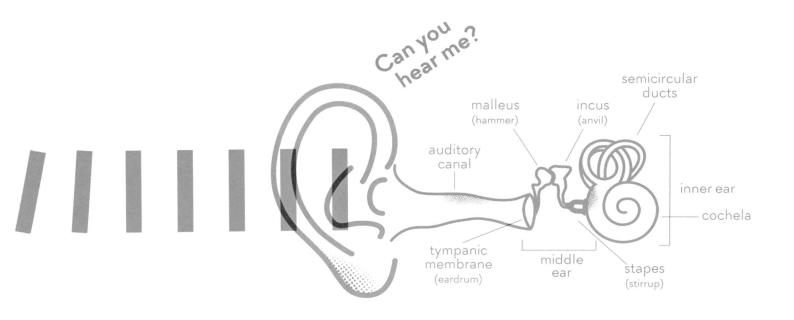

Can you
hear me?

semicircular
ducts

malleus
(hammer)

incus
(anvil)

auditory
canal

inner ear

cochela

tympanic
membrane
(eardrum)

middle
ear

stapes
(stirrup)

**Sound is usually invisible. But it attracts our attention,
we listen for it—and then, we hear it.**

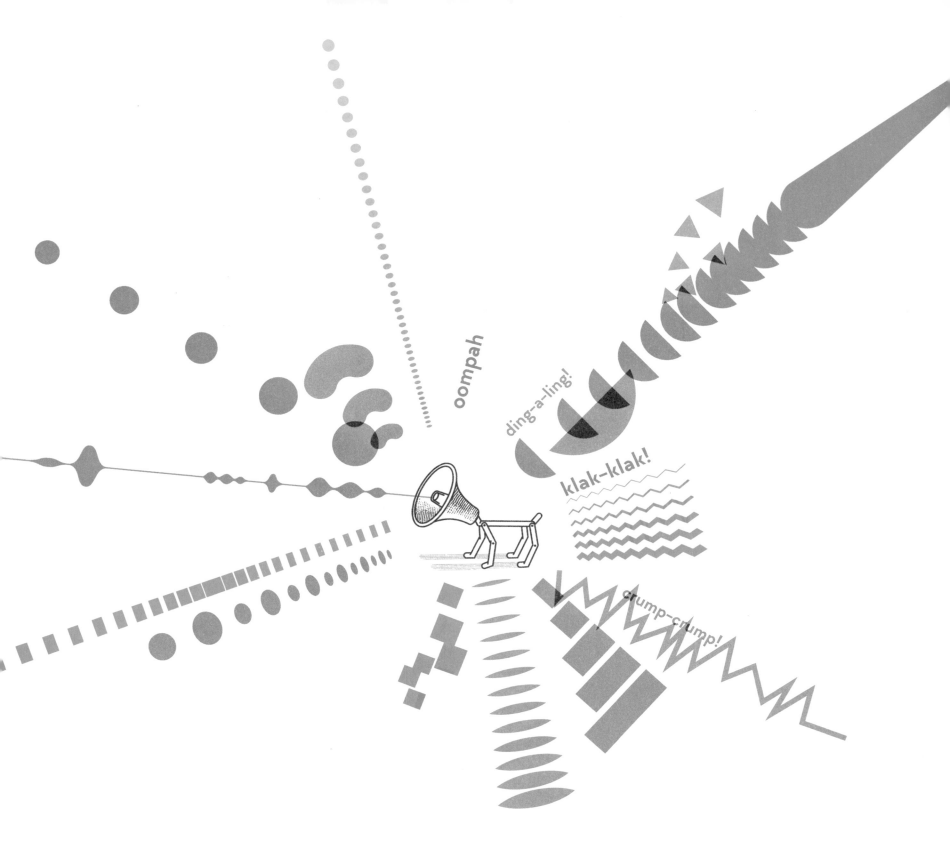

oompah

ding-a-ling!

klak-klak!

crump-crump!

There are so many different sounds:
loud and soft, high and low, familiar and new.

p piano (softly)

harp

pan flute

violin

viola

cello

double bass

In the sea of known and unknown sounds,
we look for order and harmony. This is how music is born.

saxophone

rainstick

clay whistle

twee – twee

organ

accordion

mouth harp

trumpet

French horn

xylophone

drum

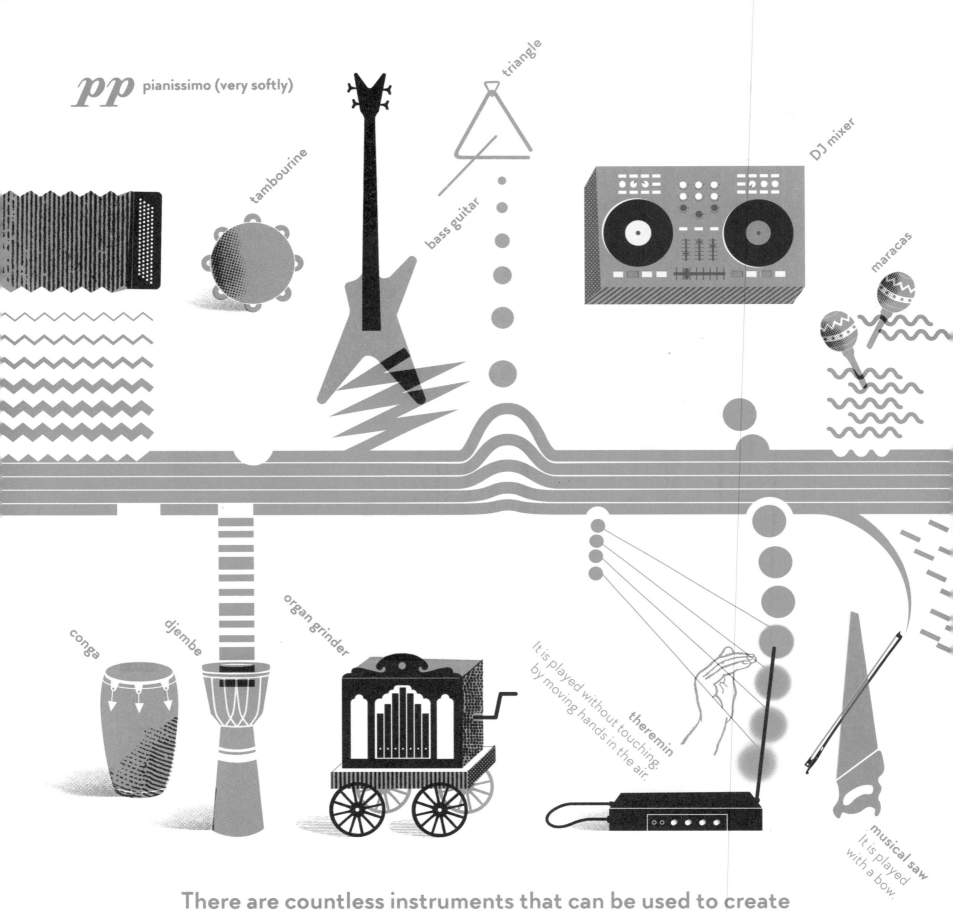

pp pianissimo (very softly)

triangle

bass guitar

tambourine

DJ mixer

maracas

conga

djembe

organ grinder

theremin
It is played without touching,
by moving hands in the air.

musical saw
It is played
with a bow.

There are countless instruments that can be used to create music—some simple, like the drum; others complex, like the organ.

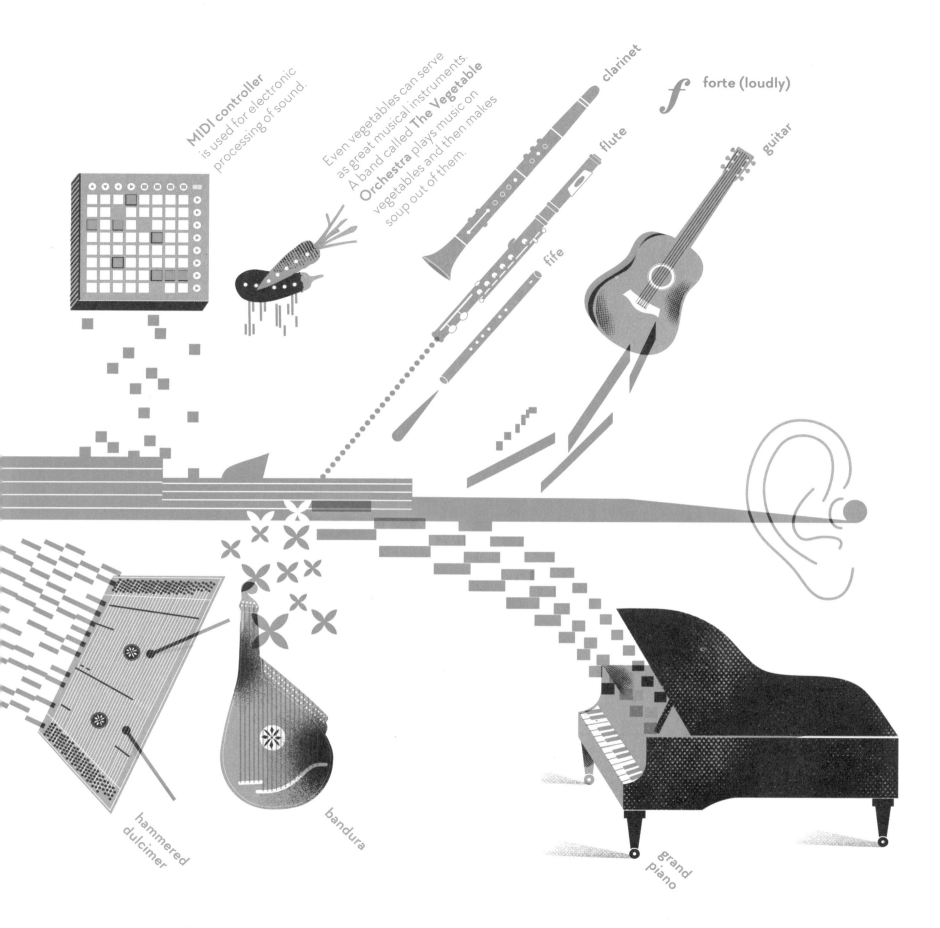

MIDI controller is used for electronic processing of sound.

Even vegetables can serve as great musical instruments. A band called **The Vegetable Orchestra** plays music on vegetables and then makes soup out of them.

clarinet

f forte (loudly)

flute

guitar

fife

hammered dulcimer

bandura

grand piano

You can perform solo or make music together with others.

bass
low

baritone
medium

tenor
high

male voices

We all have our unique ways of sounding. This is our voice.

soprano
high

mezzo-soprano
medium

contralto
low

female voices

Voices help us communicate and understand those close to us.
And with the help of voice you can also perform a marvel that is called singing!

hiccup

sneeze

sniffle

snore

slurp

wheeze

whistle

To hear the sounds
inside our bodies,
doctors use
the **stethoscope.**

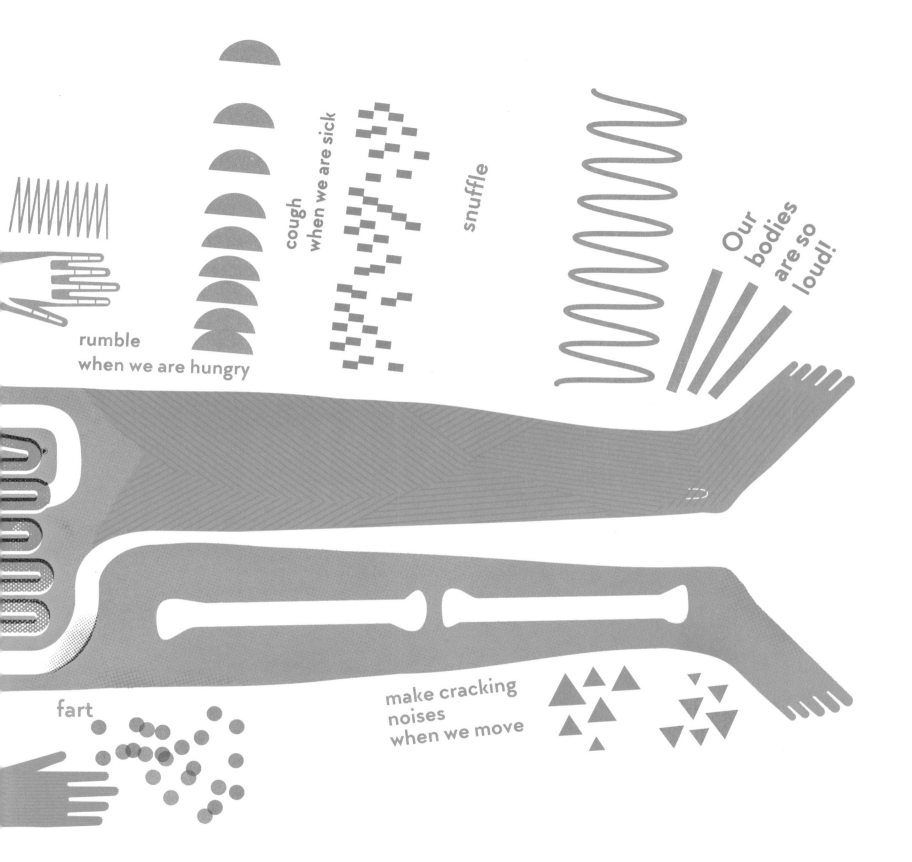

rumble
when we are hungry

cough
when we are sick

snuffle

Our
bodies
are so
loud!

fart

make cracking
noises
when we move

Our bodies perform their own music.
They create so many different sounds!

Symphonic House
On the shore of Lake Michigan,
the architect David Hanawalt and
the installation artist and musician
William Close built a house that
sounds like a musical instrument.
Inside and outside the house
there are strings, and its walls
have special acoustic properties.
The house lets wind pass through
its walls and rooms, creating
melodious sounds.

O sole, O sole mioooooooooo o   o o oooooo oooooo o o o oooooo

Our homes can sometimes sound like a musical instrument.

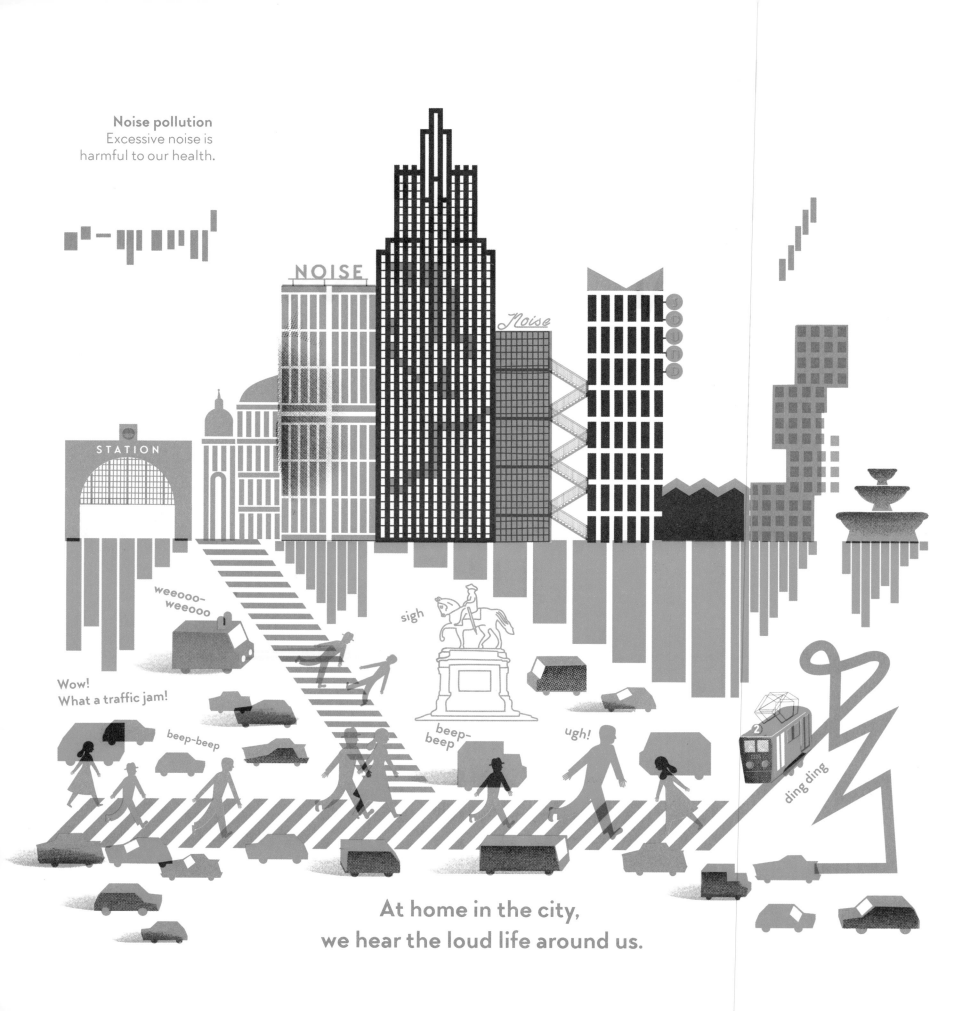

Noise pollution
Excessive noise is harmful to our health.

At home in the city,
we hear the loud life around us.

Sounds overlay, multiply, and mix together—creating noise.

The sounds of nature calm us down. When we are under stress they improve how we feel, even when we listen to them from a recording.

galumph

flap-flap-flap

chirrup

peck peck

crunch

squeak

The voice of nature hasn't changed; what we hear is very much what our great-grandparents heard. But it may seem softer because the mechanical sounds are louder and some animals have become endangered or extinct.

hoot
hoot

splash

Echo
We hear it when sound
reflects off a barrier and
returns back to us.

Some birds, like parrots, can expertly repeat the sounds they hear.

chirp!
chirp!

Crickets have ears . . . . on their knees!

So many voices on land, in the air, in the water!
Here everyone listens closely to even
the slightest rustle.

ribbit!

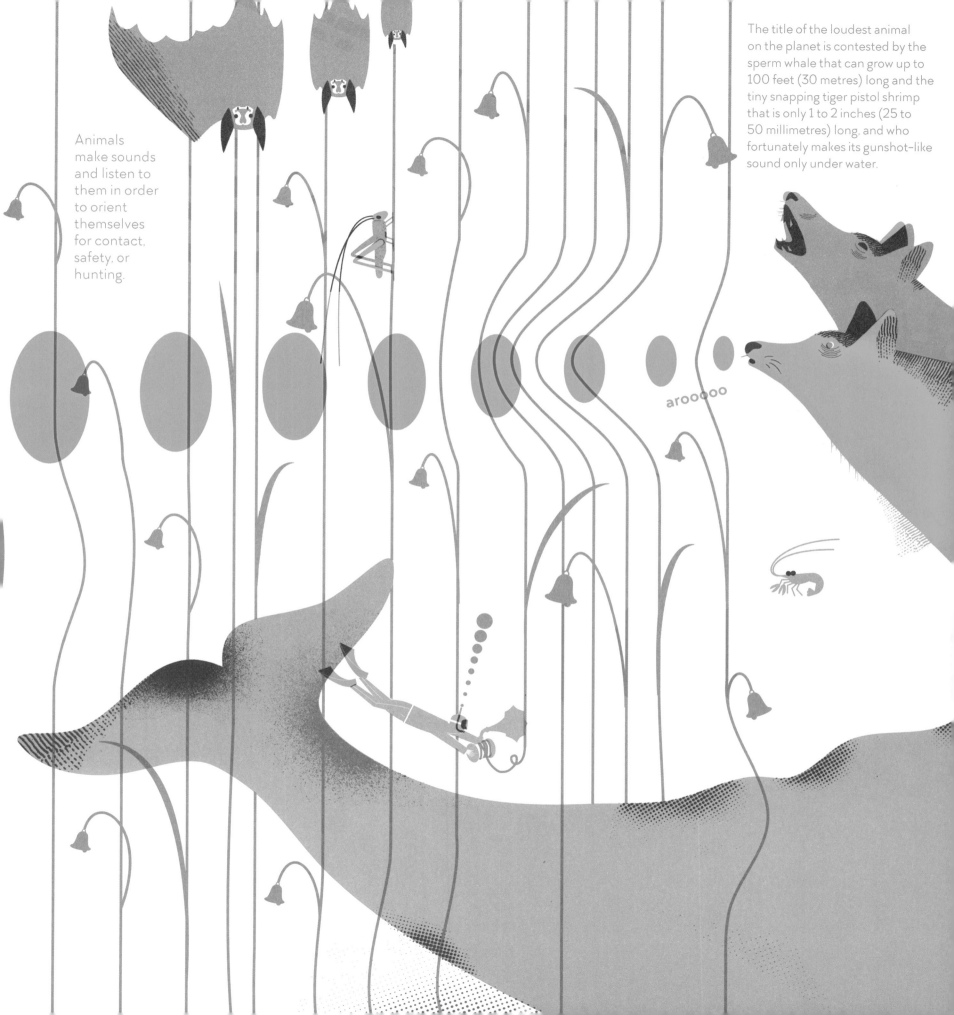

Animals make sounds and listen to them in order to orient themselves for contact, safety, or hunting.

The title of the loudest animal on the planet is contested by the sperm whale that can grow up to 100 feet (30 metres) long and the tiny snapping tiger pistol shrimp that is only 1 to 2 inches (25 to 50 millimetres) long, and who fortunately makes its gunshot-like sound only under water.

arooooo

dB

The loudness
of sound is measured
in decibels.

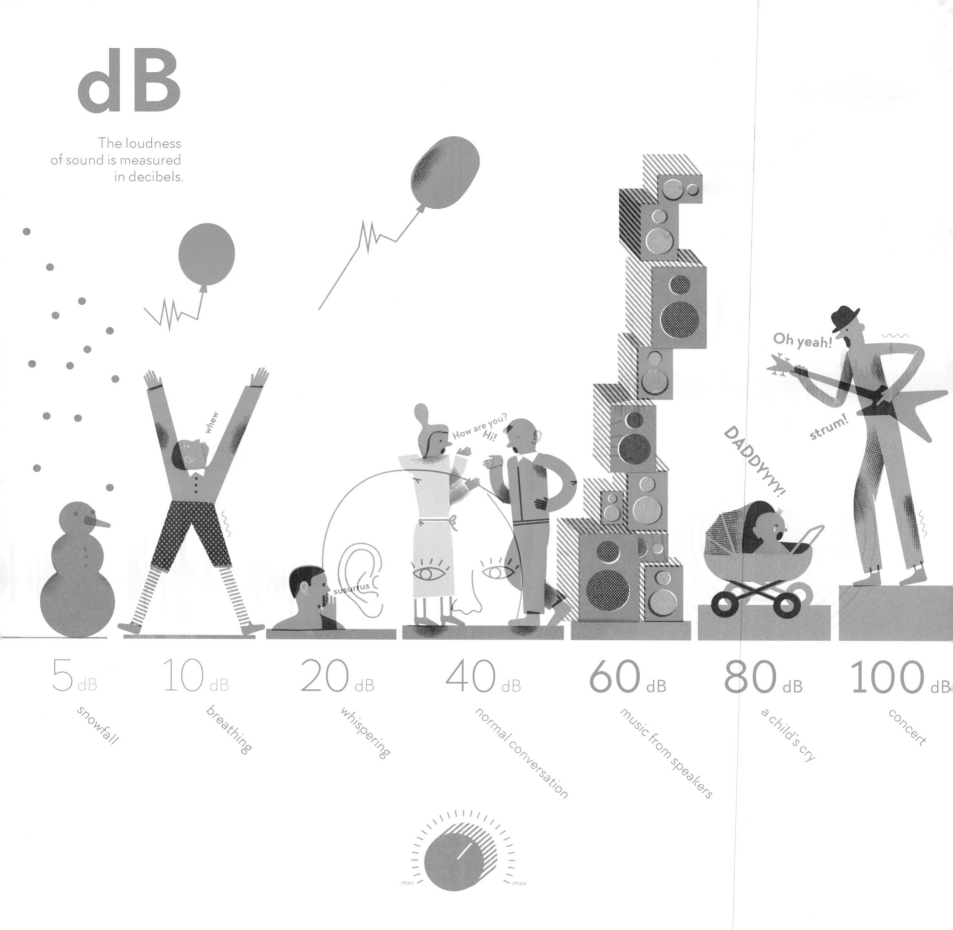

5 dB — snowfall

10 dB — breathing

20 dB — whispering

40 dB — normal conversation

60 dB — music from speakers

80 dB — a child's cry

100 dB — concert

Sometimes it is so quiet that you need to strain to listen,

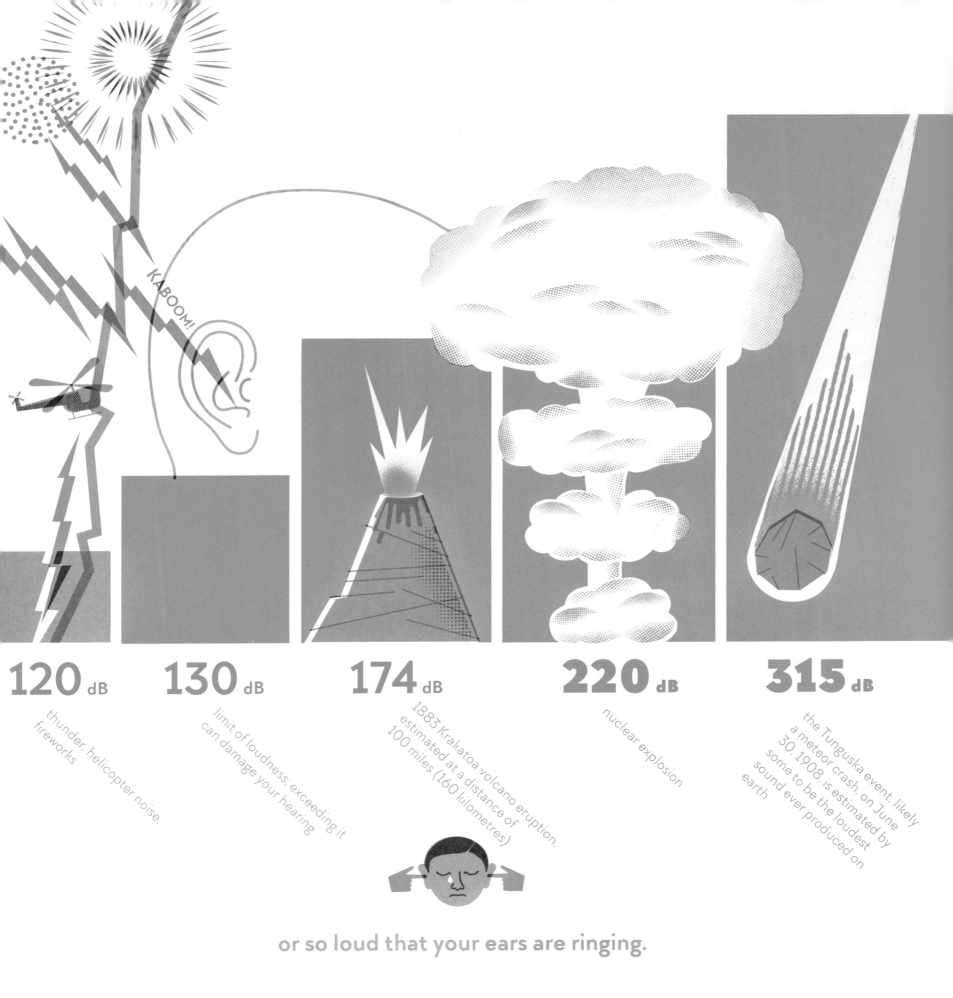

120 dB

130 dB

174 dB

220 dB

315 dB

thunder; helicopter noise; fireworks

limit of loudness: exceeding it can damage your hearing

1883 Krakatoa volcano eruption, estimated at a distance of 100 miles (160 kilometres)

nuclear explosion

the Tunguska event, likely a meteor crash, on June 30, 1908, is estimated by some to be the loudest sound ever produced on earth

or so loud that your ears are ringing.

Hz

The frequency
of sound waves
is measured in hertz
(Hz). Humans only
hear sounds whose
frequency is between
16 and 20,000 Hz.
Sound waves below
16 Hz are called
infrasound, and
above 20,000 Hz,
ultrasound.

Some of the sounds made by whales,
rhinoceroses, and elephants fall into the
infrasound spectrum.

**There are also lots of sounds that we do not hear.
But other ears can hear them.**

Echolocation
Bats "cry" in the ultrasound spectrum to orient in space.

The greater wax moth has the finest hearing among all animals.

I can't hear anything!

Whales and dolphins can communicate in ultrasound.

Some animals hear sounds in a much wider spectrum than humans.

Sometimes sounds are so beautiful that we want to listen to them over and over again. For this reason, sound needs to be recorded and preserved.

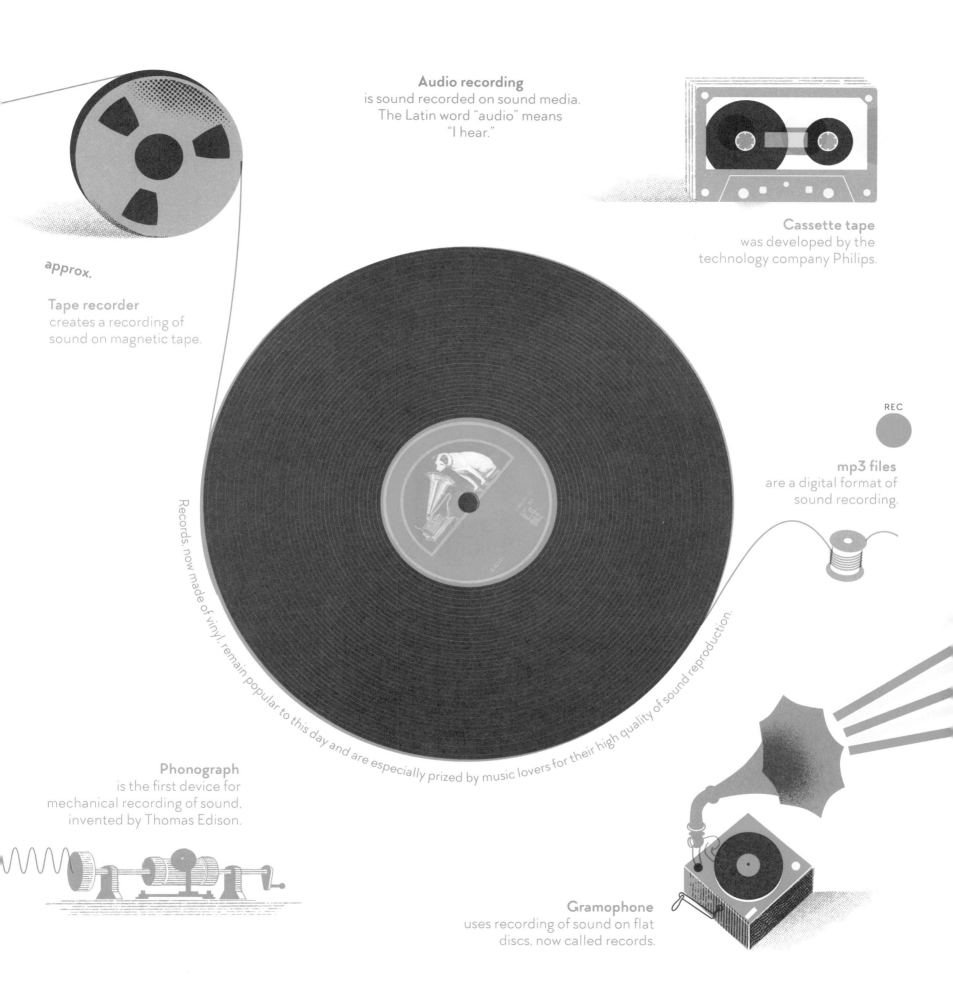

Audio recording
is sound recorded on sound media.
The Latin word "audio" means
"I hear."

Cassette tape
was developed by the
technology company Philips.

approx.

Tape recorder
creates a recording of
sound on magnetic tape.

REC

mp3 files
are a digital format of
sound recording.

Records, now made of vinyl, remain popular to this day and are especially prized by music lovers for their high quality of sound reproduction.

Phonograph
is the first device for
mechanical recording of sound,
invented by Thomas Edison.

Gramophone
uses recording of sound on flat
discs, now called records.

Musicologists
are scholars who study music and often are well versed not only in the history of music but art and literature as well.

Arvo Pärt is coming to visit!

F major

strum!

Musicians
play musical instruments and perform works of music—their own or those created by composers or other musicians.

Louder!!!

Start the rehearsal!

DJs
create music playlists for parties. They either reproduce recorded music unchanged or alter it with special equipment.

Conductors
manage the performance of works of music. The sound of the conductor's baton knocking often begins the concert.

Equalizer?

Acousticians
know everything about the way sound travels through walls or reflects from them. They work at concert halls, movie theaters, and recording studios.

la la la

Singers
are musicians who create music with their own voices.

People of sound. Thanks to them we hear much more and much better.

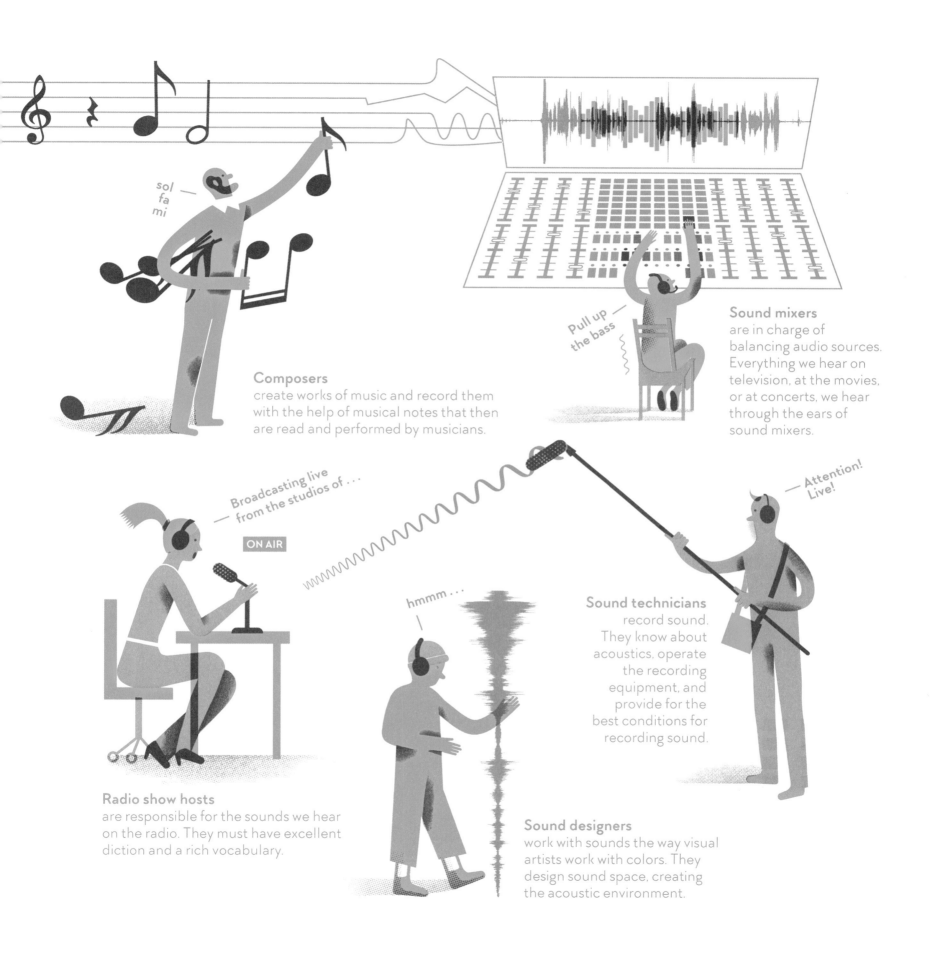

sol
fa
mi

Composers
create works of music and record them
with the help of musical notes that then
are read and performed by musicians.

Pull up
the bass

Sound mixers
are in charge of
balancing audio sources.
Everything we hear on
television, at the movies,
or at concerts, we hear
through the ears of
sound mixers.

Broadcasting live
— from the studios of . . .

ON AIR

— Attention!
Live!

hmmm . . .

Sound technicians
record sound.
They know about
acoustics, operate
the recording
equipment, and
provide for the
best conditions for
recording sound.

Radio show hosts
are responsible for the sounds we hear
on the radio. They must have excellent
diction and a rich vocabulary.

Sound designers
work with sounds the way visual
artists work with colors. They
design sound space, creating
the acoustic environment.

소리
(Korean)
sound [sori]

صوت
(Arabic)
voice [sawt]

声
(Chinese)
sound [shēng]

קול
(Hebrew)
voice, sound
[kol]

There are
more than
seven thousand
languages
in this world.

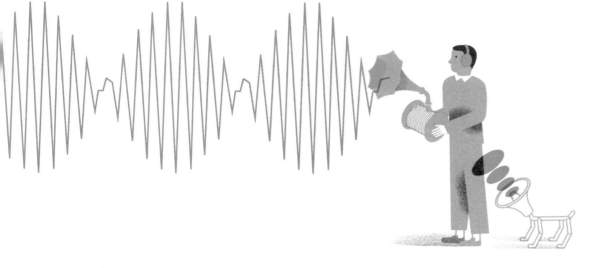

In order to understand one another, we speak.
We speak in a language. While some may seem
similar, each language sounds different from others.

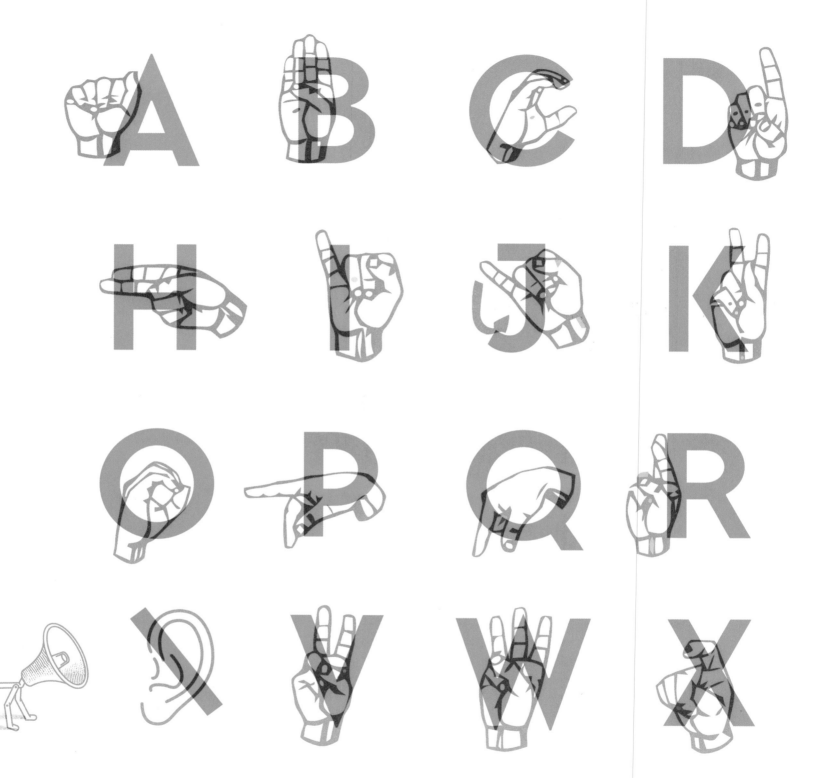

But languages are not just about sounds.
You can also understand another person in silence.

 E  F  G

People who are **hard of hearing**, or **deaf** use sign language. There are more than 150 sign languages in the world.

 L  M  N

Fingerspelling is the manual alphabet of sign languages.

 S  T  U

Sign language interpreters translate from a spoken language into a sign language and vice versa.

 Y Z

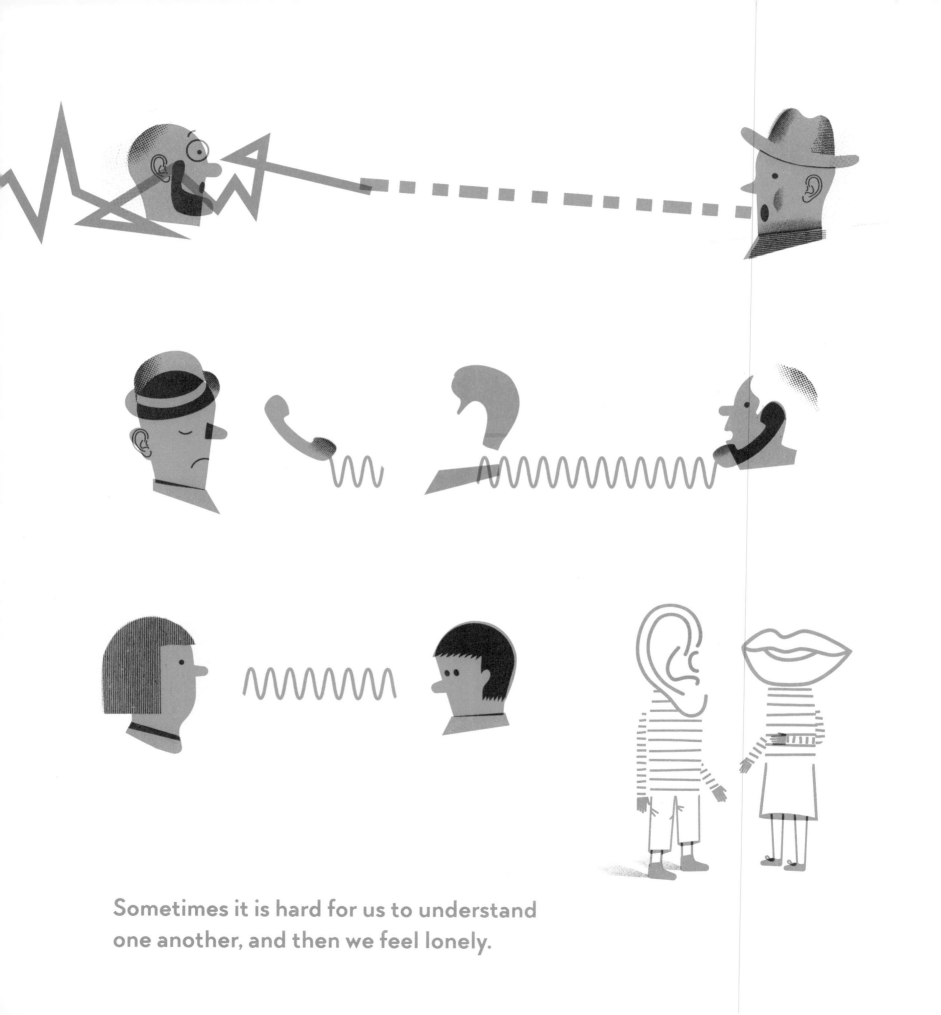

Sometimes it is hard for us to understand
one another, and then we feel lonely.

But one can find common language and understand the other person
even without words.

gh moan ticking clang ruckus boom hullabaloo fizz hiss rustle clatter chatter rataplan
runch crump squeak creak mumble rattle whimper murmur sough moan

And sometimes, we need to
spend time in silence,

murmur sough moan babble chirp rattle whimper clatter chatter rataplan clang buzz beep hiss rustle creak mumble crunch crump squeak tinkling knocking hullabaloo fizz ruckus boom whistle

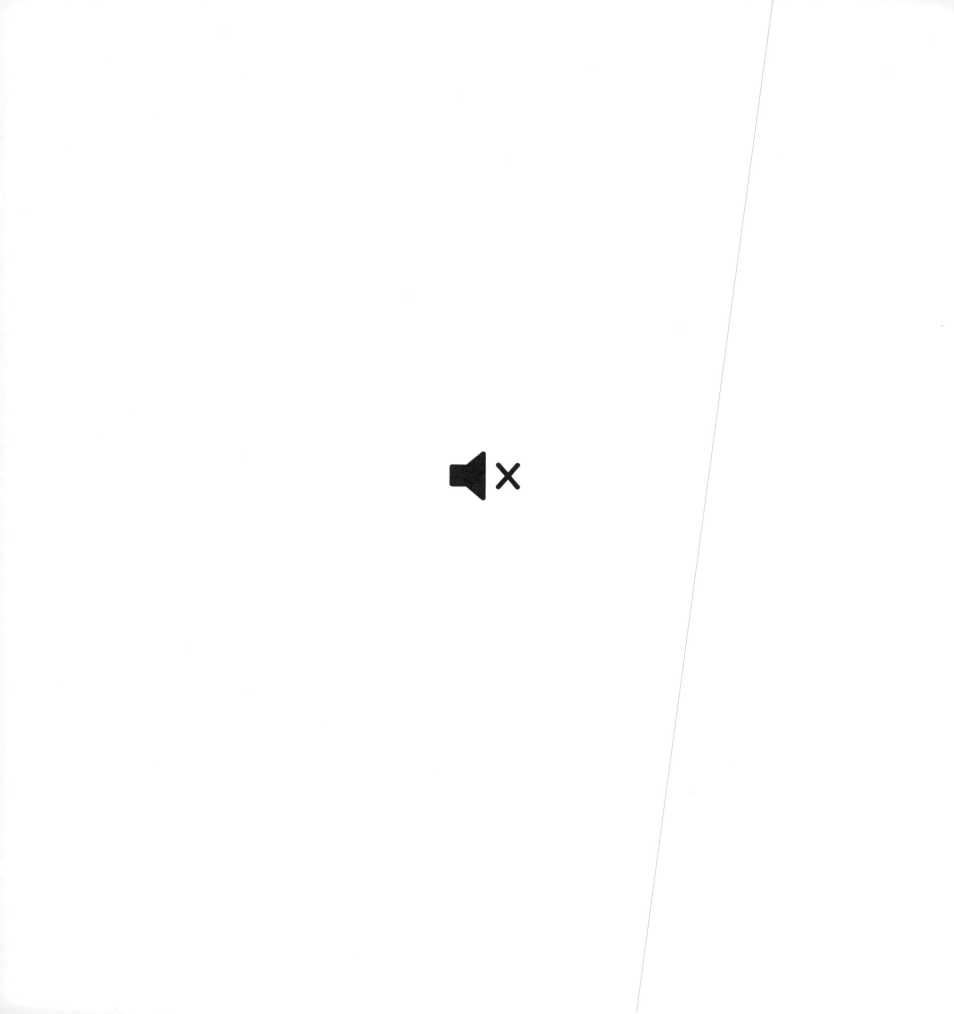

completely turning off noise,**

in order to hear the softest sounds.

Silence may let you find something you've been seeking for a long time . . .

and hear something really important—
like the sound of two hearts beating.

We hear our first sounds really early.

We begin to search for our own unique sound.

Shush

And then we learn
to listen, to hear,
and to perceive
our world.

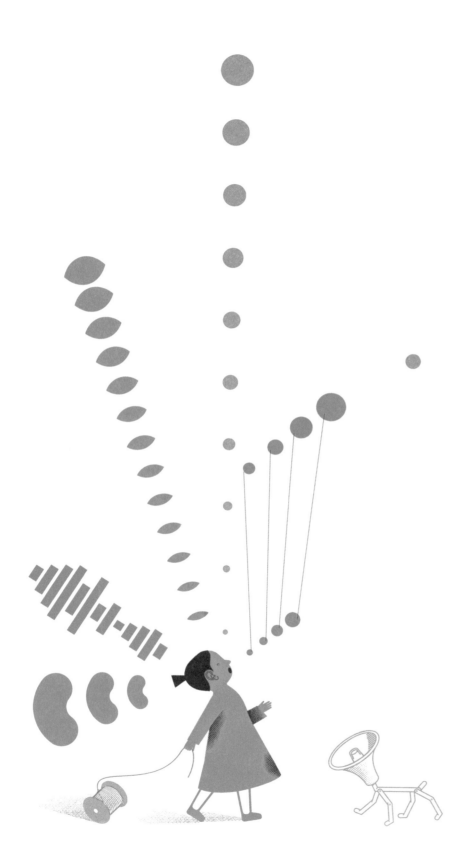

The publisher would like to acknowledge with thanks Catherine Karp for her thorough and thought-provoking fact-checking of the manuscript.

Original text and illustrations copyright © 2017 by Vydavnytstvo Staroho Leva Ltd.
Translation by Vitaly Chernetsky © 2017 Vydavnytstvo Staroho Leva Ltd.

First published in the United States of America in 2020 by Chronicle Books LLC.
Originally published in Ukrainian in 2017 under the title голосно, тихо, шепотом by Vydavnytstvo Staroho Leva Ltd. (The Old Lion Publishing House).

Library of Congress Cataloging-in-Publication Data available.
ISBN 978-1-4521-7978-0
Manufactured in China.

English language edition design by Lydia Ortiz.
10 9 8 7 6 5 4 3 2 1

A Handprint Book

Handprint Books is an imprint of Chronicle Books LLC,
680 Second Street, San Francisco, California 94107

Chronicle Books—we see things differently.
Become part of our community at www.chroniclekids.com.

Silence rules in outer space. The oldest sound in the Universe is the sound of the Big Bang. Its age is approximately 13.7 billion years, and today we can hear a reproduction of how it sounded thanks to the mathematical calculations by the physicist John Cramer.

Listen to silence: the American composer John Cage created a "silent sonata," a work titled «4'33"», it takes 4 minutes and 33 seconds and during this time the musicians just sit and do not make any sounds. It was first performed in 1952.

Meditation is the time when we stay alone with our consciousness, in silence.

Mimes are actors who without any sounds, just with their gestures, facial expressions, and body movements create rich artistic imagery.